Two Sides, Same Coin
Fictional-Nonfictional Accounts of Rights

By Kimberly A. Mucker-Johnson
Cover by Derrick A. Smith

Copyright © 2016 Kimberly A. Mucker-Johnson

All rights reserved. No part of this publication may be reproduced, stored in a retrieval system, or transmitted, in any form or by any means, electronic, mechanical, photocopying, recording, or otherwise, without prior written permission from the publisher.

Qui Docet Discit Publishing, LLC
Louisville, KY 40272
quidocetdiscitpublishing@gmail.com

ISBN: 0988816873
ISBN-13: 978-0988816879
LCCN: 2016947230

It is easier to build strong children than to repair broken men.

-Frederick Douglass

Dedication

First giving honor to my Lord and Savior, Jesus Christ. Thank you, for your many unyielding blessings! Without you I am nothing.

This book is dedicated to my grandmother, Shirley Ann Lewis Mucker, whom I affectionately called "Nanny" and my husband, Eric. Nanny never graced the halls of the university. She did not have any letters behind her name, but her wisdom was infinite. Even though, she is no longer on this earth, her legacy continues to live in the lives of those who knew her. I remember as a small child, she would constantly remind me that there are at least two sides to every story. This may seem simple, but it has allowed me to be able to see multiple sides of every story. I thank Eric, for allowing me to share his story and the internal conflict that he faced as he stood strong through the process of desegregation. I am grateful that he and others paved the path, so that many others would be able to follow.

Last, but certainly not least, I thank my two sons, Derrick and Keonte'. I thank them for continuing despite the struggle that so many African-American males face on a daily basis. Remember, someone is always watching you because you are living epistles read by men.

Acknowledgments

The great author, Maya Angelou once said, "History, despite its wrenching pain, cannot be unlived, but if faced with courage, need not be lived again." Her quote is just one of many indicating that if we do not face our past, then it could be repeated; it definitely does not need to be repeated. In fact, not knowing your history, which includes knowing and exercising your rights as a citizen could lead to an erosion of those rights. We all know what happens when something becomes eroded. Well, just put it this way, the dream that Martin Luther King, Jr. described in his speech becomes the dream deferred that Langston Hughes wrote about. It dries. It festers. It stinks. It crusts. It sags. It explodes. And when something explodes, it no longer exists. It is useless. With an explosion there is usually a loud noise, then the "deferred right" evaporates into thin air leaving behind only fragments of residue.

This book was written for any learner who does not know the history of how the U.S. Constitution played into the lives of two young citizens in Louisville, Kentucky during school desegregation, specifically during the 1975-76 school year. And how that history continues to be relevant today even though many youth do not exactly understand its relevance. The story begins in 2016 and then there are "look backs" at the past. This book is a work of historical fiction, meaning there are real historical facts revealed through a fictional backdrop.

Preface

There once was a coin with two sides. Yes, it was all one coin, but there were two sides. Now when it came to value, it did not matter which side was facing up because value is determined by the coin itself and not by any particular side showing. The problem occurs when there is a dispute or some other issue that needs to be resolved and the coin is tossed into the air. While the coin is in the air, rotating edge over edge, one side chooses heads and the other automatically gets tails. Disputes are often solved because parties believe that the solution rests in heads or tails. Many times, we are led to believe that based on probability, there are only two possible outcomes. But what about solutions that can be reached in the edge over edge movements that the coin experiences in the air.

I know you came to hear Jalen's story and to experience circumstances from his point of view, that story is coming shortly, but before we go there let me give you just a bit of history. A bit with seemingly two sides, but really multiple sides. You will see how the coin is presented from two different sides and then how it is tossed into the air, which reveals its multifaceted sides. Watch and see how everything unfolds and how it is all based on one coin.

To even write a Constitution for this new country took extensive and collaborative work; it was difficult to try to include the desires and needs of everyone in this one rulebook. It was not long before two sides of the coin emerged – federal and state, north and south, freedom and bondage.

How was the division of power to be divided between these two sides, especially when you have issues that arise, such as slavery, an issue that is not clearly defined in the Constitution?

The north and south sides of the American coin thought they had it all planned. They had managed to make sure there were the same number of free states as there were slave states. But that did not last long because as new states entered into the Union, the scales were tipped. On the one hand, Southern states wanted to expand slavery because that is how they made their coins, and on the other hand, Northern states were more interested in industries because that is how they made their coins. These disputes or coin tosses into the air led to cases such as this one:

Born and raised as a slave, Dred Scott traveled to various free states with his owner and endured a succession of multiple owners before seeking freedom for himself and his family. He launched a legal campaign, but lost in St. Louis district court. A second attempt would prove to be victorious only to be overturned by the U.S. Supreme Court. The majority of the Justices stated that he was not even a citizen and did not have a right to bring a white man to court. The decision made in this case would go down in history as one of the worst decisions that the Supreme Court could have made. Ultimately, Dred Scott was given his freedom, but he only lived about 18 months as a free man.

Taken together, all of these motives, angles, and sides would eventually lead to a civil war – a fight from within. Both sides of the same coin fighting against self. In literature, we call this internal conflict. In the middle of the civil war, Abraham Lincoln signed the Emancipation Proclamation, but not to abolish slavery as many have taught. This again was a strategy to preserve the Union. This war or self-to-self conflict would result in the loss of 600,000 to 700,000 lives, which is way too much blood to have been lost for nothing. Not to mention the fact that many children fought, bled, and died in this war, and if they happened to have survived many were left orphaned. Can we really just turn our backs on the great cost of this war?

For African-Americans, the blood bought us the Thirteenth, Fourteenth, and Fifteenth Amendments. Even though these amendments became part of the Constitution, part of the rulebook, it still would be through many trials and tribulations before we would be able to taste the fruit of so many people's labor and blood.

This book serves as a fictional-nonfictional account of the history of the above mentioned amendments. It was written because so many people count on the school system to teach their children, their history. As an educator, I can assure you that the version taught in many classrooms across the country is the clean, sterile version. It is the duty of everyone to teach the whole version not just heads or tails, but to toss the coin into the air and let it rotate while revealing multiple sides, multiple perspectives. Stay tuned as the sun's reflection illuminates varying sides and angles of this coin. Like the Jews teach their young not to ever forget the Holocaust, our young must be taught not to forget the horrific journey we have had to travel to get here. There is still much work to be done to make sure that we do not repeat the past.

This journey is about rights. It starts with the U.S. Constitution and narrows to the year 2016 where we meet an African American boy who must struggle to understand and to demand his rights. Jalen, the main character, his family, the school, teachers, and principal are fictionalized in this book, but real under various names throughout the nonfictional world. The stories, even the ones by Eric and Bern, are real accounts as they were told to this author, however some names were changed. Let me introduce you to Jalen Williams…

BALLIN'

When I'm ballin' in my hood, it's as if my heartbeat and the bounce of the ball hook up and become one.

Thump, thump thump, thump thump

As I eye the net, lift up the ball, and let it roll off my fingertips, I feel the *swish* in my heart at the very same time the ball slides through the net. All net. I could play ball all day long. I don't even mind playing by myself. It takes me away from reality at least for a moment. It helps me not to focus on my daddy and how he don't even call me or come see me or play ball with me. Bruh, I'm getting into my feelings again, my fame is suddenly interrupted by the sound of my name...

"Jalen, call it, heads or tails."

I leave the YUM Center only to return to real life where I'm met by Malachi. He trips me out with these dreads swinging from side to side. It don't help that his walk is almost like a gallop or something. But anyway, he's my dog. Always has been, always will be. He's like me, an only child, so we depend on each other. We breathe the same air.

"I call heads."

Malachi tosses the quarter into the air and it rotates, and rotates, and rotates, before falling to the ground and landing with heads up.

"Heads it is."

Good, I'm up first. Malachi and I don't talk much while we're playing. So if you walked up on us, then you'll just hear a lot of grunts, grumbles, and snorts as we man-up against each other to win. We're almost to 21 when I'm suddenly disturbed by a familiar screeching of my name...

"JALENNN!"

The first thing that comes to my mind is that she needs to quit all of that screaming, but that is quickly tucked way down because my moms don't play. Even tho it's been a few seconds since she called, I can still hear my name bouncing around ears. I swear my eardrums just got busted. Man, that really hurts my ears. Naw, it hurts my heart cause there ain't even nothing to do in the house, but look at each other. Most days, I'm on punishment for one thing or another, so when I'm able to hook up with my boy, man, I don't even want to leave.

"Here I come." I look around as

everybody stops what they're doing just to stare at me. Shoot, I don't care what they've got to say under their breaths when their mama calls, they better run in, too. I stop dribbling and let the ball roll over to Malachi's fingertips. "Man, bring the ball next time."

"Aight, I got you." He says as he lifts the ball up into the air.

I want to turn around to see if he made it, but right now I have to look at my mama's eyes cause she demands attention when she calls.

IN OUR HOOD

I live in Louisville, Kentucky. Home of Derby, which means nothing but a new fit and some barbeque in my hood. I'm in the eighth grade at Thurgood Marshall Middle School, so I don't have to go far to get an education. Even tho, I could walk, I hop on the bus every morning. Most people in my school and in my classes, live in my hood. They either live on the same street as me or around the corner. We play ball together. We all get our uniforms for school at Shaheen's Department Store. Our mamas are friends, so that means if you do something wrong then the whole hood will know about it within minutes. Maybe even seconds on a good day. My school is full of us African-American people with some other brown people mixed in. But know this, even tho every class has a sprinkle or two of salt, there is mostly pepper at TMMS. We all are walking around with almost the same story – no daddy at home and mama barely making it cause she having to do it all. All by herself.

My mama knows how to run her mouth on the phone, tho. I hear her talking about my school to her friends. I know I shouldn't be meddling, but the conversation always go the same way. She starts off saying that my school is not a good school because of low test scores. Then, she makes a comment about how our children are not getting what they need to be successful and how she wishes she could've homeschooled me. Naw, she can't wish for that cause I don't wish for that. I can only take her in small doses before I need to get up through. Her teaching me for six hours a day that wouldn't even work. After a while, she breaks down with how she wishes I could've gone to George Washington Middle School in the east end, but they said I had to go to TMMS. She usually sums up the conversation with hope by reiterating that I definitely will be bused to Waggener High School next year. Waggener is in the east end. Supposedly, that's where all the rich people live. I've heard they have green grass and concrete driveways where you can play ball. Yeah, they don't even have to go to the park to ball.

Since I've been at TMMS, I've had some good teachers, some aight teachers, and some bad teachers. Let's take my social studies teacher this year, Ms. Windows. I call her Ms. W for short. Don't let the name fool you cause she's definitely not an opening in education. She's aight, but she still needs some work on teaching.

At the beginning of school, you know when they trying to introduce themselves and meddle in your business at the same time, she told us this was her second year of teaching. And you most definitely can tell cause she don't even know what she's doing. If she gets real confused about something, then she'll go sit at her desk and work on her iPad. I hate to be the one to tell her if she's trying to find help on the Internet, that won't help. Stuff on the Internet about us ain't true. If she wants the real deal then she's gonna have to come in our hood and hang for a minute. Maybe sit down and have a glass of sweet tea with my mama while they sit on the porch and take in the air.

Ms. W's starting to get on her iPad more and more lately. It's actually making me mad cause we ain't learning nothing in this class. Then if we get bored from waiting on her to tune back in to us and we decide to talk, take a nap, or occupy ourselves in some way, then she's mad. For what? She ought to be mad at herself. When she's really mad, she'll call your mama and if she can't get your mama then she'll keep going down the contact list until she reaches somebody. Well, that somebody'll know how to get in touch with your mama real fast. Remember, I told you news travel fast in the hood. My mama has been called or tracked down at least a hundred times already this school year. And every time my mama is called, I have to hear, "Jalen, you are going to the east end next year and they definitely will not put up with your behavior." Put up with my behavior? I ain't putting up with their behavior.

I keep telling Mama I didn't even do anything and then I spread my arms out in front of me with my palms up while my shoulders are hunched up. I don't know where I got that from, but that seems to go with, *I didn't even do anything.* Ms. W is just picking on me. I don't understand why she has a problem with me cause I didn't even do anything to her. Whenever she asks me if I learned anything, I tell her the truth by replying with a big, fat **N-O**. And if you're dumb that spells NO. She can't expect us to sit in a seat all day and do nothing. Why? What's the use in even coming to school if I can't hang with my friends or even sleep if I need to cause I'm tired sometimes?

WHAT'S RELEVANT?

Every single day, Ms. W has been pounding into our heads what she calls the **rules of the land**. She acts like it's so important to HER that we learn this stuff. She probably want us to pass some test or something. That's all they think about – *the test is in May, this will be on the test, you'll need this for the test.* We already have low test scores, so it don't even matter to me. I mean, what does what happened then have to do with what's happening now. NOT A THING! Let's think about this…a bunch of white men got together and made up some rules way back in 1780 something. How is that supposed to even be important to me in 2016? It's not! I won't be listening to what she's got to say because I have other things to do. Why didn't they come up with some rules about how black boys are being killed in the streets or how about how we can't even trust the po po because they keep turning up corrupt? How about some rules about how my mama has to struggle to take care of me while my father runs the streets because he can't get no job? Here she comes again over to my seat.

As soon as she gets to my desk, she leans over and starts messing with me with this stupid whispering, "Jalen, I have noticed that you haven't been paying much attention to the lesson today on the Constitution. Do you already know this stuff?"

"Naw, this stuff's boring. When we gonna get to what's happening now? I mean, that's over 200, probably going on 300 years ago. I ain't got no beef with them, and they ain't got no beef with me. They dead ain't they? Well, dead men don't have nothing mo to say." I ended my explanation with a few fidgets in my seat and shuffles of my papers. Well, really I just moved some of the papers on the bottom to the top to make it seem like I knew what I was talking about. Like I was prepared. Like I was the defense attorney. Somebody had to defend me and I guess it was me. So there.

She just stares at me as if she ain't impressed with my opening statement, so I start thinking real fast about something that I could ask to convince her that I'm trying. I lowered my voice and made it sound like Thurgood Marshall back in the day, "Huh…I read that first part before. You know…that beginning part that says *We the people.*"

First she seems disturbed that I changed my voice, so she just stares and stares as if she needs to recover her balance. Then she shifts and re-shifts her weight from one side to the other, "Oh, so you know the Preamble to the Constitution?"

"No, I didn't say that I knew it. I just said that I heard it all before. I think they said something like that on a TV show or something."

"Ok, Jalen so let's go to page three and I want you to read the Preamble; that's what the introduction is called, read it to me and explain what it means in your own words." She jumbles these directions together so fast as if she's trying to lose me in the translation stage.

At this point, I knew I had gotten under

her skin, but at the same time I knew I was busted, and I didn't need her calling Mama again today. So I turned to page three and began reading in my Jalen voice, *"We the people of the United States, in order to form a more perfect union, establish justice, insure domestic tranquility, provide for the common defense, promote the general welfare, and secure the blessings of liberty to ourselves and our posterity, do ordain and establish this Constitution for the United States of America."* **Swish. All net.** After I was done reading, I noticed that she was smiling, so I said, "What you smiling for? I know how to read. What? You didn't think I could read or what?"

"No, I am perfectly aware that you can read. I just like how dignified those words sounded as they rolled off your lips. Even though that is just the Preamble, those words are so important to being an American citizen. So what do those words mean?" She puts her hand on her hip as she waits for me to respond.

I'm thinking to myself, *wait for it, wait for it, wait*, and then the silence stands up like he about to take over my thoughts. He just wants me to admit that I don't know what I'm talking about. I have a silent exchange with him and then I put Ms. W on blast, "I don't know what that mean! Leave me alone!" I drop the ball because I don't even feel like playing no more.

It seemed as if a light bulb came on in her mind because she shifted into gears ready to break it all down for us. She was like a coach, spewing out plays before the final buzzer. I had already fouled out so I was only half listening. As she was trotting back to the front of the class, the bell rang. Saved by the bell! It was the end of that class. I smiled because I knew I had just escaped any further punishment on learning about them old, dead people that don't care nothing about me.

UNTAPPED VS. TAPPED OUT

As soon as I got home, I filled up on TV before Mama got home cause I'm on punishment again cause of the last time Ms. W called home on me. She's the only one calling. She keeps saying over and over that I *have a lot of untapped potential.* Whatever that is supposed to mean. I believe that I am all tapped out. Really tho, I feel that I am tapping into everything I got just to make it to school every day. Just to sit through her class is a win for me.

Since mama won't let me watch TV, I'll be asking her to tell me a bedtime story when she gets home. Last night, she told the story about slaves and how they were treated on the plantation. That story didn't do nothing but make me mad. Mama said I shouldn't be mad cause we won. She said enduring such devastation and still surviving is a win. Tonight, she promised that she would get to the story about the octoroon. This should be interesting.

Around 8:30 PM, I hopped into the shower, lathered up, rinsed, and dried. I'm only in the shower five minutes at the most cause if that soap dry up on my skin, it'll make me itch like crazy. I put on my jersey and some shorts and climb into bed.

Mama walks into the room as she's twisting her hair back into place for tomorrow. "How my baby been doing?" I don't mind her talking the baby stuff in private, but if she ever do it in public then I'll act like I don't even know her.

I muster up the best *I-gotta-sound-*

believable smile that I could, "I been doing good. Now, can we get to the story, please?" I knew that I had better add *please* or Mama would reprimand me for talking slick. She's been telling me stories ever since I can remember, but I never discuss this with my boys. What happens in the Williams' home, stays in the Williams' home.

She sits on the bed and looks at me eyeball to eyeball as if she's staring a hole right through me and then she switches gears and rephrases the question, "I'm just checking on my little man. How was your day?"

First of all, I ain't little no mo. I ain't little J. I'm big J. But I know I better not be disrespectful. My mama can't handle disrespect. As she turns her head slightly to grab another bushel of hair, I rephrase my answer, but momentarily forget how to say it without using street talk, "It was aight."

Her neck jerks around and she drops the last twist that she was working on, "It was ***aight***? BOY, what I tell you about talking like that."

I quickly self-correct before this gets out of hand, "I'm sorry. I mean it was alright. Ms. W made me read out loud." I said as I tried to redeem myself by making mama believe that I'm doing what I'm supposed to be doing at school.

She must've forgotten about the last twist that she was working on because at that point, she gave me her undivided attention, "Good. So let's get to the story of the octoroon:"

Homer Plessy was an octoroon. The best way to remember the meaning of an octoroon is to think about other words that start with 'oct' such as octopus, octagon, and even October. You see, at one time October was the eighth month of the year, but that's a different story. Anyway, an octoroon is a person that is 7/8 white and 1/8 black. In other words, their great grandparents consist of seven whites and one black. Homer actually looked white, but people knew his racial lineage and there was a pesky, little rule back then that said if you had one drop of black blood in you then you were considered black. Remember, I told you that things were separated back then. There were 'white only' trains, water fountains, restrooms, schools and there were 'black only' things. So, in 1896, some people that were against things being separated, hatched a plan. Since people considered Homer to be black, then he would purchase a train ticket and sit in the white only car. This was his way of demonstrating civil disobedience for his rights.

I suddenly became interested and confused at the same time cause I understood what disobedience meant. Mama's been preaching that word to me for over a decade, but I didn't know what civil disobedience was. "Huh, Mama what's that?"

"What's what dear?" Mama said as she moved her face closer to mine.

"Civil..I mean I know what disobedience mean, but not the civil kind."

"Oh, I'm sorry. Yes, civil disobedience is when you think something is not right or unfair and you protest without violence or cursing or acting a fool. You just decide to resist almost passively. But really, it isn't passive because people know that you are actively demonstrating."

I think she just confused me even more, but my ears opened up as I became more interested. I tried to digest this info in my head and tried to figure out exactly how this civil thing works, but all I could come up with is it must be a way to be disobedient nicely. I can do that! Wait, I better ask what happens when you disobey in a nice way.

"Well, what happened to Homer when he refused to go to the 'black only' train car. Did they beat him like in *Roots*?"

"Not that I know of, but we'll never know the whole story. However, he was arrested and convicted for not obeying the law. This was all part of the plan, so that he could file charges."

> *So he went to court for breaking the law and Judge John H. Ferguson found him guilty. He wasn't happy with what the judge said, so he filed charges on the judge and went to the Supreme Court. You see, Homer felt like he wasn't being treated like a citizen and that he didn't have equal protection of the law. The Supreme Court ruled against Homer because they said that separate could be equal. This really hurt the feelings of Homer and a lot of black people because they knew that separate could never be equal. Their eyes had been showing them for years that separate wasn't equal. At black-only schools,*

the building was run down, textbooks were worn out, and there was barely food. Even, the black-only water fountains, were not in good shape and the black-only train cars were simply not as nice as the white-only train cars. Anything that was black-only was not as maintained, new or in as good of shape as the white-only versions. Yet, they wanted blacks to just accept what they had been given and accept their reasoning behind it. But there would come a day when all of this would come to a head and the chickens would come home to roost.

It seems like after she said those last few words, my eyes must have rolled into the back of my head because I was out. First, I started dreaming about mad chickens coming back home. Then, I dreamed of a man that was divided into eight parts with seven parts shaded white and one part shaded black. Next, I was on the court all by myself jumping into the air, performing a layup when the ball was knocked out of the basket, and I was suddenly jolted back to reality by that familiar, at-times-screechy voice, "Jalen, get up and get ready for school."

Here we go again.

CIVIL DISOBEDIENCE

Having Ms. W first period just puts me in a bad mood for the rest of the day. When we entered the classroom, Ms. W was sitting behind her desk studying her iPad. Without taking her eyes off the screen, she said, "Make sure you get out your vocabulary notebook and copy the terms on the board."

Sure enough, on the board was them words from the Preamble that she didn't get a chance to explain yesterday. I knew she would continue this today.

Word	Meaning
union	joining
justice	fairness/equity
tranquility	calm
defense	protection
welfare	well-being
liberty	freedom
posterity	future generations

After the bell rang, she announced, "Class, these are some words from the Preamble, which may be unfamiliar to you. Let's go over these words."

She spends the next few minutes talking about these words and their meanings. I am bored, bored, and BORED. Closing my eyes, I began thinking about Homer Plessy and what it must have been like to be only 1/8 black. Can you image being split into eight different parts and seven of those parts were white and one was black. That sounds deformed to me. My mama and my daddy are both whole black and that makes me whole black. The thing about it is that Homer looked like a white man and that must have been cool because when you want to be black you can, and when you need to be white you can. Oh I forgot again, that wasn't the case back then cause just one drop made you all the way black. Suddenly, my thoughts are harassed by Ms. W standing over me again.

"Jalen, I know you aren't sleeping in my class?"

"No Ms. W, I was just thinking with my eyes closed." The class broke out in laughter. I wasn't even trying to be funny. I watched as Ms. W's face transformed from pale pink to girl pink to fire red. I thought carefully before speaking and when I thought I had gathered enough words to speak I said, "Ms. W, I wasn't being just plain disobedient. I was exercising civil disobedience because I have already told you that I don't care about them dead men that created a bunch of rules. Instead of getting mean about it, I've decided to think about more important matters like how black people have gotten treated in this country.

So I don't wanna fight with you, I'm just going to think about mo important issues."

She hardens her face and twists her lips as she forces each syllable, "Why Ja-len Wil-liams, you have just told me that you are not go-ing to o-bey the rules of my class. You think that you can sit here and sleep and re-fuse to pay at-tten-tion. That will not work, young man! Since you have fail-ed to learn these words on my time, then you will need to learn them on your own time. To-night for home-work, only Ja-len will re-write the Pre-am-ble in his own words and then he will pre-sent his pa-ra-phrased ver-sion to the class. You got that young man?"

"I got you." I guess civil disobedience don't work cause she seemed to be just as mad when I did it civilly as she would've been if I'd been just regular disobedient. Oh well, some people never win. This was just a losing season for JW. I better do a good job on this homework or she may call my mama. I don't need her calling my mama because she's already taken the TV away and I ain't seen Malachi in a minute.

MY BUSINESS

When I got home, Nana was there. That means that Mama would be working one of her jobs overnight. I love Nana, but sometimes she can be all up in your business. I run up to Nana, plant my head in her chest, wrap my arms around her stomach, and squeeze her real tight. She bends down and kisses me on top of my head. It's one of those old people kisses. You know the real wet ones that makes you want to wipe away the excess.

I remove my backpack and sling it onto the kitchen table, "Nana, I got a lot of homework to do." I was just letting her know that I didn't have time to tell her all my business today.

"That's a good thing. That means they teaching you something over at that school." She says as she continues stirring something on the stove.

"Whatcha cooking? Cause I need me some energy b'fore I do all this work." I drop my body into the seat and make my head fall limp to give the impression exhaustion.

She turns around, stares at me, and smiles. "You are just a growing that's why you need so much food. Boy, I'm cooking as fast as I can. Didn't you eat lunch at school?"

"Yes ma'am, but that's been a lonnnnggg time ago. And I could only eat a little bit cause that stuff don't look like what they be saying it is. Like today they said it was hamburger, but that couldn't been no burger."

I pull out my notebook and flip through the pages. All the pages are blank. I hadn't even written down the vocabulary words from the Preamble. Uh oh, I'm in trouble now. I didn't write down the words and I wasn't listening to the discussion. Oh well, I guess I better tell Nana that I need to get on the computer for my homework.

I jump up out of the chair and head straight to the computer in the living room, but then it dawns on me that I forgot that quick to get permission first. I run back to the kitchen chair and raise my hand to get permission to talk. Nana does not play. When Nana notices my hand is raised, she nods her head. This means that I can speak, "Nana, I need to get on the computer for my homework because I have to write the

Preamble in my own words."

"Boy, you better get on that computer and use it only for studying. I better not find you on there playing a game or doing any other foolishness. That's why you ain't allowed to play on the computer now or watch TV because you always into something that you shouldn't be." She shakes the big spoon at me as if she is reminding me that it could become a weapon if need be.

"I know, Nana, I know. I'm going to do right. This is a big test grade, so I have to find this info." I march into the living room, pull the chair out, and jump in. I talk myself through how to find stuff on the Internet. I remember that I could go to dictionary.com to find out the definitions, but I need to look up the Preamble first and print it out.

Nana cooked some chili. After I read through the Preamble and pulled out all of the words I didn't know, it was getting late. There was a lot of words that I didn't know. Most of those abstract nouns are hard to understand. I ended up stopping for only 15 minutes to shove a couple of bowls of chili down my throat and then I went right back to work. This was one of those long games that goes into overtime, but you have to keep playing your best cause there's still a chance you might win. When I finished my homework, it was already past 11:00 PM. I didn't feel like taking a shower so I put on my jersey and shorts, hopped into bed, and snored my way into the world of sleep.

1975

Next thing I know, this teenager with these weird flared blue jeans, a cross between a crew and turtle-neck shirt, Converse tennis shoes that were way out of style and an afro shows up. Well, his afro didn't bother me as much as his outfit. It looked old. Like, where you from old.

"Bruh, who are you and what is you doing up in my room?"

He just stares at me and then he finally talks, "What's up, my name is Eric and I'm here to take you on a journey back to 1975."

"1975? Dude, for what? I ain't going nowhere. Do you know how many years back that is? My mama was born in 1981 and she's old."

"Look, you little eighth grader, you are definitely in need of learning something about your history because you refuse to learn it in class. I have been sent to make it a little more real for you. You sit in school and half pay attention to your social studies teacher and then you wonder why no one is doing anything to help black people in 2016. Well, one way that you can begin to help yourself and other black people of today is to learn your constitutional rights."

"Why you keep saying black people? We call us African-Americans today. Our skin ain't even black! I hate when people do that. Shoot, that's dumb!"

"Jalen, you know what I am talking about." And as soon as the last word escaped his lips, we were sitting in front of a TV at some old-timey house.

"Where we at?"

"Shhh…listen to the news."

> *Many parents and community leaders are upset about the violation of their rights by forcing busing upon them. With Louisville being the largest school system to take on desegregation, many are looking back at what happened in Boston last school year.*
>
> *About three years ago, Boston public schools were found to be racially imbalanced, so all schools with more than 50% white enrollment were required to be racially balanced. This court-order affected the entire city. The start of school was delayed by a week because of all the necessary pieces that needed to be added to the*

puzzle. While the newspaper boasted of a great opening day, the real opening included black students greeted by bricks being thrown at their buses, signs hanging from buildings that said, "Nigga Go Home", pictures displaying monkeys, and spittle and hate being spewed from protesters' mouths. Other than these minor issues, the media boasted of having a "generally peaceful" start. That's one side of the coin. The other side, the black students that endured such hate, referred to their experience as a war zone. Although black students didn't feel safe, they still showed up for classes, however the white students refused to come to school. Attendance was at an all-time low. Desegregation was definitely in the air.

While only four miles apart, South Boston and Roxbury were worlds divided. Many say these two schools should not have been coupled together for desegregation purposes. That maybe, just maybe, it would have been easier to desegregate schools that were not so different, but it had already been done.

I unglued my eyes from the news and turned to look at this Eric. For a few brief minutes I couldn't even form words. As I scanned Eric's 1975 living room, looking for my guide's eyes to inform me of why he made me learn about this horrible history, I couldn't help but feel sick. I kept looking and looking for Eric, but I couldn't find him.

Next thing I know, I heard my mama yelling, "JALEN, GET UP! IT'S TIME FOR SCHOOL."

ENCOURAGE YOURSELF

We together are America and in order for this relationship to be perfect, we must have fairness, peace, protection, and care about everyone. This is for us and future generations.

There you have it – short and sweet. No one will ever know that it took me til 11 o'clock last night to figure all this out. I took a bow and returned to my seat. The class applauded me, but I was only looking at Ms. W's face to see what it told. Other than turning red, it said nothing. It was blank. It didn't applaud. It just stayed almost plain mad. She acted like my paraphrasing was nothing more than an act of punishment. I told myself, *You did a good job, Jalen,* as I patted my own back. To me, tho, I'm the underdog but I had just won. Mama said there are times when you have to encourage yourself. I guess this is one of those times. Besides, I'm used to her not complimenting me on anything, so I had to quickly learn to ignore her and to compliment myself. Anyway, she only notices the bad.

As my butt hit the seat, Ms. W began talking about the seven articles of the Constitution and I began thinking about desegregation in Boston that I had watched on Eric's old timey TV. At first, I kept pausing the video in the back of my mind. You know the one showing how black people were treated back then. But then I would turn around and push play all over again. I kept trying to coach myself through this game called life. I told myself that I had to focus because it would help get my mind off of those pictures of monkeys, but it wasn't going to stop without a struggle. I wrestled with the inner Jalen, but apparently he had seen too much because he seemed stronger than the outer Jalen. He

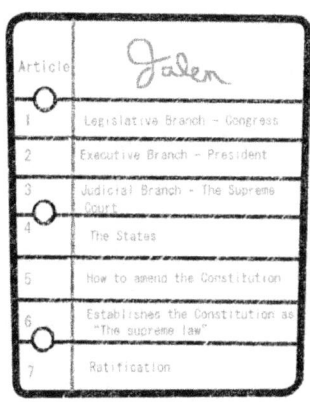

picked me up and tossed me. I rotated from heads to tails, tails to heads. Eventually, the inner Jalen just fell flat on his back and, the outer Jalen was able to push stop. But I could tell that he was bruised. Very bruised.

   I picked up my pencil and started writing down all the facts that Ms. W was sputtering. I didn't really understand all the articles and stuff, but at least this time I wrote down some information. So I guess the Constitution is like a magazine with articles in it. Each article is on a different subject, telling a different story that somehow fits into the whole. Ms. W showed us how to write an article months ago. I wrote my article on basketball and how to dribble. I remember getting a big, fat B on that assignment and she didn't even tell me why I didn't get an A. I know for a fact that I should've gotten an A. Suddenly, my thoughts were confronted by the word "test". I don't know what came before or after, but apparently we're going to have a test. Oh well, she'll be aight! I don't even know why we're going over this anyway.

FROZEN TEARS

Mama began telling me a story called Frozen Tears. It was about a black family that tried to enroll their little girl, Linda into a school that was only four blocks from their house. The problem was this was a white school, so the people at the school said, "No, your child cannot enroll here". Linda had to walk seven blocks to catch the school bus and then ride an overcrowded bus for more than two miles across town to attend the black school. This left her mother devastated with the reality that her little girl experienced bad weather when walking seven blocks. In fact, Linda said at times, she was so cold that her tears would freeze right on her face.

In Topeka, Kansas, black people lived all over town, but could only attend black only schools. This was found to psychologically damage the black community. It was time to take this to court and it eventually went all the way to the Supreme Court.

For a moment, I forgot that I wasn't at school. I began to raise my hand to ask my teacher, I mean my mama, a question. She paused and looked patiently at me, "Mama, did you say Supreme Court?"

"Yes dear, the Supreme Court."

"I think, I mean, Ms. W. was teaching us something about the Supreme Court." I said as I eye searched for my backpack.

"Well, what did she say about the Supreme Court?"

I knew this was coming and I knew that I couldn't make up something fast enough, so

I proceeded down the court with caution then I said, "Aww, they are part of the articles."

"That is correct, they are part of the articles." She bent over and kissed me on my forehead. "Goodnight, baby. I love you." I love the softness of her voice when she isn't mad at me. I nestled down into the mattress and closed my eyes. Immediately, my eyes popped back open. Wait a minute.

"Mama, you didn't even finish the story!"

She paused at my door and turned around, "Well, the story ended with the Browns winning, so schools weren't allowed to be separate anymore. Black children and white children could go to the same school because separate could not be equal. This seemed to some to be a small win, but years later it would come to be seen as a huge victory not just for public schools but for society in general."

"Mama, these stories you be telling sound so real", I said and as I shuffled my body further down into the mattress. I didn't wait for a response. Next thing I knew, Eric had grabbed my hand and was transporting me back to 1975. AGAIN!

TALE OF TWO SYSTEMS

"You just can't be showing up whenever you get ready. Mama just told me a story and I was getting comfortable." I said as I tried to make my hand small enough to escape his grasp. I managed to get it loose at least for the moment.

He stopped and gave me a look and then said, "Little boy, you don't know."

"Know what?'

Eric grabbed my hand and said, "You don't know where you came from, so you can't know where you're going." Next thing I know, we were sitting in a classroom.

"Aww man, why you bring me here? I'm already in school and I don't like the stuff Ms. W puts out. You gonna bring me to school in my sleep. C'mon, I'm going back to my bed"

He inserted his hands in the pockets of my shoulder and guided me to sit in a chair. The next thing I know it's like a movie is being played.

> *Over 40 years ago in Louisville, Kentucky something changed. This something would change public education from that day to this one. Up until this point, this city had been divided into two school systems – Louisville Public Schools and Jefferson County Public Schools. The Louisville Public Schools were the city schools, which is mainly where black students attended. The Jefferson County Public Schools were the schools located in the suburbs and*

this where white students mainly attended. In April 1975, these two systems became one. While this merged over 130,000 students under one school district called Jefferson County Public Schools, this move didn't racially balance the schools.

Well, you're probably wondering what's the big deal with making sure schools are racially balanced? Well, it all comes down to the fact that when schools are not racially balanced, there's an issue with the quality of education and resources being equal. There's a problem with everyone receiving a quality education. Apparently, there had been some federal lawsuits put in by civil rights groups concerning these here schools in Kentucky. And apparently, this had been going on for four years. And apparently, there was some opposition from school administrators, who had been appealing the federal suits put in by the civil rights groups. Well, long story short, it all came to a halt on July 30, 1975. Federal Judge James F. Gordon ordered full desegregation of all Louisville schools. His order was accompanied by a plan, which he made public at that time. Beginning the 1975-76 school year, which began on September 4, 1975, approximately 22,600 students were bused. White students would be bused for two out of their 12 years of schooling and blacks would be bused eight or nine years.

All school enrollments were required to be at least 12 percent black, but no more than 40%.

COUNTED

I kept trying to keep my head up in school the next day. I'm just so tired. Too much information. Too much history. Eric's field trip was extra. In between yawns, I heard something about the Amendments. I look around my class and notice that it is segregated. *Wait*, I thought about it. Jefferson County Public Schools was desegregated in 1975! Then why are there only three white students in my classes – Scott Thompson, Katie Schultz, and Laura Keeling. See, in middle school, you are on a team and you travel all day with the same group of students. I scan the classroom to make sure that I haven't missed anyone and then I tried to think real hard to make sure that nobody was absent. No, everybody was here today. I counted again and again, but I kept coming up with only three. I hadn't noticed before that desegregation didn't work cause how is it this many years later, there are still more black and brown kids in my classes. I'll have to ask Eric about this later.

SHOW ME

"What sup, E! I'm glad you showed up. That news reporter said that we desegregated in Louisville in 1975. Well, I counted the white people in my class and there's not that many. In fact, there's all of three. I thought there wasn't supposed to be more than 40% African Americans at a school. Well there are 20 out of 23 black and brown kids in all of my classes – that's more than 40%!"

"J, slow your role! You are just going on and on. You don't even have all the pieces yet. Let me show you my story:"

> *Raised up in Louisville's west end,*
> *I lost my dad when I was only three*

years old. He died from the complications of a car accident making my mama, a single parent of six children. I was number 4. My mama took care of the white people's homes in order to provide for us. When she came home from work, we took great care not to cause any extra trouble. Plus, mama did not play games with us. If we even thought about acting up in school, at church, in the neighborhood, then we could possibly face brutal and I mean brutal punishment. You know, that stuff that they call child abuse these days. Well, it wasn't child abuse when you needed to be disciplined for misdeeds. I was afraid of my mama because she put the fear of God into all six of us, so I did my best at school. Dude, all those calls home that you've had, wouldn't have happened in the Johnson household.

By now you are probably wondering what this has to do with desegregation in Louisville, Kentucky. Well, it has a lot to do with desegregation because the thing about it is respecting others starts at home. You see, hate is a learned behavior. People don't just hate for hate's sake. They hate because they have been taught hate most likely by their parents. So, when all this desegregation stuff came on the scene, I had to withhold many of my feelings because my mama wasn't hearing it. She didn't want to hear that we were being taunted. She didn't want to hear that we were treated differently. She only knew that she wanted her children to have a better education and she thought that could only happen through busing. She believed leaving our neighborhood would expose us to a different way of living like she was being exposed to every day while she cleaned those white people's homes and cooked their dinner.

WHO WE WERE

My public education started at Henry Clay Elementary. Oh, I mustn't forget to mention that Henry Clay is now known as Young Elementary. It seems like there was always all black students in my classes except for Darryl. He was always the only salt among the pepper in class. So this is how we flowed through school, from Henry Clay Elementary, we went to Russell Junior High (for one year), then we went to Shawnee Junior High, and then we went to Shawnee High School. All of our schools were right here in the city, in our neighborhood.

When I got to the tenth grade, rumors began circulating that change was coming. Apparently, somebody decided that all of us, city kids, were going to the county for school. And some of the county kids would come to the city. The thought of this did not sit well with me. I kept wondering who had the bright idea of busing me for 30 minutes or more when Shawnee was almost literally in my side yard? Not to mention, Shawnee was a way of life for the Johnsons. Heck, let's just call it a family tradition since I was the fourth Johnson to attend Shawnee High School. My sister, Jackie and my brother, Tony had already graduated. My sister, Sherry was one year older than me, so she *was in the 11th grade at Shawnee. My younger brothers and I had come up through the ranks from Shawnee Junior High. Now I was in the 10th grade and since this Johnson tradition had already been set, I didn't think there was any need to change. Graduating from Shawnee High School was a given for me. It was what I desired and expected. It was the neighborhood school. It was who we were.*

Darryl didn't have a problem being the only white student in our classes and we didn't have a problem with Darryl. Just as I thought I was safe, somebody snatched my expectations away from me. Somebody changed the trajectory of my future. Whoever they were, I didn't like what they were putting out. As the thought that I would be the first Johnson to attend and graduate from one of those county, east end schools crept into mind, I grabbed the thought and arrested it. Mmmm...I hate to throw a monkey wrench into these plans, but I'll be attending and graduating from Shawnee. Go east end for what?? That summer, it would be the news and my momma that would have the final say.

I yawned and rubbed my eyes as I woke up. Awww shoot, I done fell asleep at school again. Ms. W is standing up at the board teaching on the Amendments. She don't even make eye contact with me. I guess she tired of dealing with me, but I'm tired of dealing with her and her boring lessons. She mentions something about the Second Amendment and then she realizes that I'm woke, "Jalen, since you decided to join us would you explain the Third Amendment?"

"Bruh, I don't even know. I'm tired."

"I'll tell you what, go stand out in the hall and I'll be out there momentarily."

I drop my pencil, stand up, pick a swagger, and walk out into the hall. As I'm standing in the hall, I can hear Ms. W finishing her lesson on the Amendments. I try to listen, so I can keep up for this big test that's coming up. My attention becomes divided as I listen in on the other social studies classes. I can hear Ms. Harris' class working in groups talking about the Constitution and stuff. We're already passed that, but it seems they're having more fun learning it than we did. Mr. Nason's class is watching a video on Brown versus the Board of Education. That's Malachi's class. I spot him and those dreads, he's all into it. I can't even get his attention. I remember Mama talking about the Browns, but Ms. W didn't even bother to go over that. Suddenly, I saw the frozen tears again on little Linda's face. I guess that must have been a real story after all. After what seemed like all day, Ms. W came out. Based on her expression I knew this wasn't gonna turn out right cause she had a look of disgust on her face. You know that look people make when someone has farted and it smells real bad, well that's how she looked. It's actually fun to fart and make someone look like that. I've done that so many times on the bus. I was doing it at home, too, but Mama told me that the next time I farted around her that she was gonna get me. I tried to explain to her that I couldn't help it because science says that we fart at least 14 times or more a day. But she must've known that I was forcing some out on purpose.

"Jalen, I just feel that there is something going on with you at home. I want you to know that you can talk to me about it. I've noticed that you are sleepy all the time and…well, I know that your mother is a single parent and maybe she can't make sure that you go to bed on time. I mean, who is watching you at night to make sure that you are cared for."

I stare at her for what seemed like an hour and then I tried to calculate what Ms.

W was really trying to say. It didn't seem to be adding up. She got this disgusted look on her face while she's acting like she trying to help, but she's talking about my mama not doing good with me. I was getting ready to talk real mean and bad to Ms. W for talking about my mama, but I knew I couldn't win. I needed a timeout, so I dropped my head to try to calm myself and then I said, "My Nana put me to bed. That ain't why I'm tired. I'm tired because you can't teach. Yo class b-o-r-i-n-g. You don't even like children. So why you teach?" I could tell that I was getting louder and louder so I tried to bring it back down, but it must have been too late because Ms. W turned all kinds of color and yelled murder. Then she grabbed my arm. I jerked away, "Don't be touching me, you ain't gotta touch me." She called security. Mr. Smith showed up to escort me to the principal's office. The secretary directed me to have a seat. I can hear Ms. W running me down to the principal. When she came out, she wouldn't even look my way. She just held her head up high and pranced out of the office. Mr. White, the principal, came out after her and coldly told me to go sit in his office.

"For what? I didn't even do nothing."

"Boy, who told you to talk? Go sit down!"

I didn't trust this man and I didn't trust Ms. W no more. I slid off the seat and found another seat inside of Mr. White's office. He came in after me and closed the door. It was something about the way he closed the door that didn't feel right to me.

"Ms. Windows told me everything that

has been going on. You consistently disrupt her class and then you question her authority. This means you are out of control, boy. You're behind in your work because you never do your homework and you are always off task. She also told me that she has tried to work with you and your mama, so that as a team we can make sure you get your education. Yet, it sounds like you prefer to stay dumb. You're lucky that paddling has been taken out of school because if it wasn't, I would paddle you right now. That's what you're missing at home a good paddling from your daddy. I've called your mother and she said she'll try to get off of work to come and pick you up. I am sending you home for a few days because we just can't tolerate your disruptions." I sat there as if a frog was in my throat. My outside looked as if I didn't care, but on the inside I was raging. My tears had frozen on the inside because of this inclement weather. My heart started dribbling faster, faster, faster with bad layups in slow motion. Pieces of ice kept trying to squeeze out of my head and eyes but I wouldn't let them. I couldn't let them. They were not going to make a mockery out of me. They were not going to see my rage. They were not going to see the weak side of Jalen. They had not earned the right to see that side of me. I would have to man-up and play ball. All they saw was badness in me, so all they were going to get was the frozen side of me. I had a decision to make. Should I let them see what they already believed was there? Or should I show them something different?

BROOM OF RACISM

When Mama's face met my face, I knew the star player had just let the whole team down. During the ride home, she didn't say a word and I didn't know what to say. It seems my mouth had already gotten me into deep trouble. I slid down in the passenger seat of the car and just stared forward. I knew if I said something I could possibly get knocked in my mouth. At this point, I wanted to keep all of my teeth, so it was better to remain silent. I do have the right to remain silent.

I wanted Mama to coach me and ask me what happened, but she didn't. I took that as meaning she believed what they said at school, so I didn't have nobody on my side.

It was me and the ball. No team. No coach. Nobody.

Hot dogs and pork-n-beans were placed in front me, so I ate my food and went to my room. As I laid on the bed, I kept looking at the ceiling, searching for answers to all of these questions that I have. I tried to stay woke just in case Mama decided to come in and tell me a story. Next thing I know I was sleep because Eric showed up.

"E, I just don't know. I don't know why we get treated so bad. Mom's mad. She won't even talk to me. She didn't even ask me what happened. She believes them over me. Everybody is against me."

"You know you're like a little brother to me, right? J, we're going on all these field trips so that you will learn your rights. I think it was the great Dr. Martin Luther

King, Jr. who said a right delayed is a right denied, but I believe that our rights are delayed and denied because we don't even have a clue what our rights are. I need you to pay attention to the rest of my story because at some point we will find the right key to unlock your understanding, Bro."

> *During the summer between my tenth and eleventh grade years, the news began to spread like wildfire. But as for me, my spreading was more like peanut butter on bread. The more peanut butter I spread, the more the bread ripped away. It was going to be a rough ride. The thing that scared me the most was that all the adults in my life were silent on the issue. Before school let out, the black teachers at Shawnee pretended it was*

business as usual. They did not utter, mumble or for that matter mouth a single word to confirm, deny, or reject the rumors. In fact, I think they didn't know what to make of the situation. I just knew that this couldn't be good. Good for what? Being hated because of the color of your skin? I had already lived that life, so why was I being tortured just to create an image, a façade to prove to the rest of the world that blacks and whites could go to the same school. They didn't want us out there and we didn't want to be out there. We had our own school, so there was absolutely no need. Such thoughts only infuriated me and made me feel some kind of way as fear swept my mind with the broom of racism. I shook off such thoughts because I had already made up my mind...I wasn't going anywhere! I was forever going to be white and gold!

DIVIDED WEST

I wiggled in my seat while Eric continued on. I kept thinking to myself this brother is long-winded.

> *I remember the letters filled the mailboxes on my block. The letters told our parents what schools we would be assigned to starting in September. It was weird because if you lived on the west side of 36th Street, then you were assigned to Central High School. But if you lived on the east side of 36th Street, then you would be attending Waggener High School. Well, I lived on 32nd Street, so that made me destined to*

Waggener High School. Can you believe that they actually managed to divide the West End into a west side and an east side? I was being forced to go to Waggener High School. Now that I think about all of this, I have no idea how I came to know so much about grown folk business because my mother believed that children stayed in children's places and this was grown folk business.

Mama never discussed her opinions regarding this decision. She did not look disappointed, sad or even seem nervous. I don't know if it was because she was a praying woman and nothing was going to shake her faith. Or maybe, she believed that this was for some greater good and that her children would get a better education. Whatever the reason, Mama didn't seem to flinch, and I knew that she had made up her mind that my little brother and I were going to Waggener High School.

At home, all the routines of starting a new school year were normal. We got what few new clothes and supplies my mother could afford. However, the difference happened at the bus stop. Everyone seemed to be nervous, unsure of what was going to happen. Someone said we needed a plan, so plans were devised so that we could protect ourselves if need be. One person said, "If they do something to me then it's on." Then others announced that we needed to stick together. Yet others like me just listened and contemplated what to do when something happened to us. As we stood there, more and more teenagers gathered at our bus stop and before we knew it we had 60 or more teenagers standing at our stop. People had decided not to wait at their own stops, but they wanted to be with others that they could connect and discuss the impending events. When the bus finally pulled up, everyone could not get on, so there was a scattering. Some people went back home, others caught the city bus, and yet others waited for a second bus. I secured a seat on this first bus.

Inside the bus, we were introduced to our bus driver, Ms. Barker, an older white woman. She immediately began to bark out commands such as, "Sit down!" "Be quiet!" "Stay in your seat!" "Sit up". It wasn't long before David Buckner gave her the nickname of "Ma Barker" and we all started calling her by this name. Not out of affection, but out of respect because she took control of her bus and she didn't seem the least bit nervous about delivering us to the school that didn't want us.

Upon turning into Waggener, we were met with a few white folks holding signs. I don't recall what the signs said because I had already prepared myself to block them out. Exiting the bus and walking inside of the school was accomplished without incident, but once inside we were met by the fingers. A bunch of pointing fingers directed us to our classes. No names, no welcome, no faces...just strangers with pointing fingers.

Even though my homeroom teacher, Ms. George, seemed pleasant enough as she passed out schedules. I couldn't help but sit quiet as it dawned on me that I would not be graduating from Shawnee High School. I had actually been disconnected from the school that my older three siblings had attended and graduated from. No more white and gold. Even though I was just a teenager, I somehow knew this was going to be messy, grueling work, especially when I realized that the students that had been at Waggener already had built relationships with the teachers. But for us, the teachers were strangers and foreigners.

While my younger brother (the one right under me), Kevin, went to Waggener at the same time that I did, my brother, Phillip, the baby of the family was bused to Fern Creek. When he came home from school on that first day, he told us about all the protesters that were at Fern Creek and how they threw things at the buses and called them names. It was just like it had been on TV. As we watched the news, we learned that there were several schools that had these sort of issues, so the National Guard was assigned to ride on every school bus until things calmed down.

Many of my records never made it to Waggener, which impacted my senior year. The black seniors were told that they were missing numerous course credits. Some people argued and refused to retake classes that they had taken at Shawnee. But when I was told that I was missing a science credit, I doubled up because my goal was to graduate on time. Good thing I did because out of 12 to 15 black seniors only seven actually graduated on time. The others were given some "credit missing" excuse and they were required to attend summer school. Their graduation would be in the summer, which consisted of being handed a diploma at a later date.

I guess in a way, I was one of the lucky ones. As I walked to the podium to receive my diploma, I suddenly felt the effects of having a praying mother. All in all, the "Waggener Experience" had been a smooth ride with just a few bumps, but I'd made it.

SPARED SCRAPS

I woke up late on Wednesday morning. I thought about all the problems other blacks had to endure just to go to a desegregated school. I thought about how schools have supposedly been desegregated for over 40 years, yet some of them don't even look like it or feel like it. I groaned and I shifted from one side to the next. This stuff is hard.

I could smell bacon and eggs being cooked, so I hopped out of bed. I opened the bedroom door so I could peek out and make sure the coast was clear. I didn't see mama, so I slid into the kitchen. Nana was in there singing as she flipped the bacon over in the skillet. She was singing something about overcoming when I interrupted her momentum.

"Good morning, Nana."

"Good morning, Baby. How you feeling?"

I thought in slow motion because I didn't know what she meant. I'm sure Mama has already told her the whole story and I'm sure she's on everybody else's side. So finally, I came up with an acceptable answer, "After getting some sleep, I think I am doing better than I was yesterday."

"So is that true what they said about you?" She lays the fork on the stove and diverts her eyes in my direction.

I drop my head, making sure our eyes don't connect. I can't lie as the tears thaw and drop in slow motion like water does as it is thawing from an icicle, "No, ma'am."

"Huh? What you say, Jalen? You allow yourself to be accused for something you didn't do? What were you thinking? Why didn't you respectfully speak up for yourself?"

"Because they had already decided I was guilty." Now, tears began to rush to my eyes. I didn't want to talk about it no more. I didn't want to get all in my feelings, but I couldn't hold my rock exterior no more. I wanted to go back to 1975 where I could just observe. I wanted to disappear since I'm invisible anyway.

"Well, I understand where you're coming from, but we will be addressing this here issue with the principal. We can't just let this thing go down like that. We deserve an explanation for why he made the decision to put you out of school." She paces around the kitchen for a moment before realizing that breakfast has started to burn. Then, she rushes over to the stove and salvages as much as she can. Putting the spared scraps on a plate, she sets it in front of me. As if by remote control, she paused for a brief moment, my Nana was gone somewhere else.

OTHER SIDE OF THE COIN

"Whoa dude, what you doing?" I said as Eric grabbed me and transported me back to 1975.

"You have to see the other side of the coin."

"Bruh, why you keep talking in code? What coin? What side? What are you saying, bruh?"

We landed in someone's back-in-the-day living room, but it wasn't Eric's living room. There were photographs of white people scattered all over. Then some white teenager showed up out of nowhere.

I slowed down my heartbeat and looked for my guide, "E, where are we and who is this?"

"Well Jalen, this is Bern and Bern this is Jalen."

She reaches out to shake my hand. Reluctantly, I put my hand out only because I decided not to be mean. "Hi Jalen! Nice to meet you. I've heard so much about you and how you're getting ready to go to the ninth grade at Waggener in the fall. Eric told me that you needed a little history lesson. So, I'm gonna tell you about my family and my point of view during the 1975 desegregation of schools in Louisville."

"Well, it's not…" Just as I was about to reveal that I hadn't requested to hear another desegregation story, Eric grabbed the back of my head and made me shake my head yes.

EAST SIDE

Bern mirrored my nod "yes" while she started telling her story.

> *In the O'Connell family, there was my dad, mom, five brothers, one sister and me. My parents invested in the education for the boys in the family, but my sister, Mary-Ann and I had to attend public school. See, the O'Connell boys went to Trinity High School while my little sister and me were spending our junior high and high school careers right here in the east end of Louisville at Waggener. Although Waggener was a stone's throw from our house, we rode the*

bus to school. We loved our school, mainly because we had grown up with many of the other kids. When new kids would come to our school there was a feeling of uncertainty because they were strangers to us. Before desegregation, Waggener had only a few minorities, but we didn't think anything about it. It was just the way it had always been. Nothing new.

The summer before the 1975-76 school year, there were lots of talk on the news about desegregation. I didn't pay much attention to it and there were not any family discussions about it. It was my senior year, and that's all I thought about. I was excited because I was graduating and I was going to be an adult. My mom wanted me to go to the University of Louisville, but I wanted to go directly into the work force. I wanted a j-o-b. I wanted my own life, and that life would require my own money.

The stress was made apparent on the first day of school. It seemed like as soon as Mary-Ann and I wiped the sleep from our eyes, my dad started talking real fast. It was as if all the news reports suddenly became real for him at that very moment. He kept muttering something about driving us to school as he paced back and forth. I had never seen my dad so fearful. His emotions arrested our excitement and released nervousness and fear. I didn't dare ask him, but I wondered to myself, WHY?? What in the world was

I missing in this whole situation?

Daddy coached us as he drove, "If anything happens, well you just walk right out of that school." All I could say was okay as I still wondered on the inside what exactly he thought was going to happen. Are things really that bad that he had to drive us to school? As we approached the school, I began looking for signs of potential problems. There weren't any. It was the same Waggener. I didn't see anything that was different.

As Mary-Ann and I hopped out of daddy's car, I remember he reminded us again to walk out of school if anything happened. I quickly forgot his words because on this day after attending Waggener since 7th grade, I *was walking in as a "big person". I was a senior. Once inside, I noticed that Waggener was different. There were many different faces of people who I hadn't been going to school with practically all my life. At that moment, I was able to connect the potential problem that daddy was referring to with the reality that was before me – there were many black people who had been added to my graduating class instead of just the regulars.. I could tell that some people did not like this. In fact, I chose to pretend it was business as usual because we were familiar with the teachers and the teachers were familiar with us.*

    We made it back home safe and

sound. The TV was chatting about how other schools had problems and even violence, but not at Waggener. My daddy was back to his normal self of sitting in his green arm chair and reading the paper while at the same time, listening to the news on TV. It was as if it didn't matter to him that there were protests at Jeffersontown High School; those parents didn't want their children going downtown and they didn't want black students coming to Jeffersontown. His children were allowed to stay in the east end, after the potential hiccup bypassed, it was a regular opening day of school. We had school as usual. My classes were normal. My teachers were normal. For us, the culture was normal.

Waggener was not tainted because of the entrance of different faces. In fact, our perspective of the world and other people became richer because of the diversity. My sister, Mary-Ann would end up marrying an African-American man and they would create beautiful biracial children. That's how much our perspective changed. They were people like we were people.

As soon as Bern finished her last word, "people", we thanked her, said our good-byes and we were off to one of Waggener's classrooms. E started acting like a teacher lecturing while I sat in one of the desks. I was his only student, but I needed his help.

CONNECTING DOTS

"Ok J, now that you have some real life perspectives on desegregation, I need to connect some dots for you, so that you'll be ready for the big test coming up in Ms. W's class. Remember when your mama told you about Homer Plessy."

"Yeah, I remember, but what does that have to do with you, Bern or even some test?"

"Bro, you've totally been missing the fact that everything that has been coming into your gates lately has been to prepare you for something big. Dude, IT'S ALL CONNECTED! The things your mama has been teaching you through storytelling, the lessons that Ms. W has been teaching.."

"Teaching…she ain't been teaching me nothing."

"Ok, well the few things that she has been talking about. The field trips that I have been taking you on. Even your Nana's song, has a lesson in it. It all works together to make you into a better person."

"I like the way that I am. I have swagger. I'm good-looking. I –"

"No, I'm not talking about those surface level things. I am talking about a change beneath the skin. Look dude, exposure is education. You have been exposed to all of this to make a difference in the world. Somebody somewhere is counting on you to make a difference for them. Some little kid somewhere is watching Jalen and expecting you to show him a different life. They already see the hood. They know poverty.

They know how it feels not to have a dad. There is probably some first grader or second grader or third grader or fourth grader or even one of your peers to prove that we black males are not what they make us to be. We are smart. We can think. We enjoy learning even when they don't make learning engaging for us. Look Jalen, in 2016, I'm in my fifties; yes I can be a role model for youth, but by you being closer to their ages, they'll listen to you before they listen to me. They need you; we need you to allow your light to shine in the world, and don't let no one dim that light."

    I cupped my head in my hands as I thought about all that had just happened. I couldn't argue with E because everything he was spitting was 100%. It's scary letting my light shine cause every time I do, it's met with disappointment almost hostility and then I become the bad person that they already thought I was rather than the good person I know myself to be. "E, you're right go on. Go ahead and school me some more."

ABOUT A COIN

The American government began under the Articles of Confederation. They weren't interested in a central government because they had already experienced that in Britain and didn't want any parts of that. The Articles left the regulation of slavery in the hands of each state. Many people claimed to hate slavery, but they had slaves of their own, particularly in the southern states because they needed slave labor to continue to prosper in agriculture. No one was going to give up their power and riches just to let a black man go free. I mean think about people in general. People can be quite greedy and we all know that the love of money is the root of all evil. They've been teaching us that in Sunday School since I was just knee high. Eventually, this way of governing didn't work because it didn't unify the states. So, some meetings were held to develop what became known as the Constitution.

As Ms. W was trying to tell you, the Constitution was signed in 1787 and yes, it was a bunch of white men who framed it. The Constitution was organized into three parts: the Preamble, the Articles, and the Amendments. The Preamble is the introduction. Although the Preamble was not officially part of the Constitution nor can it be used to *determine decisions on laws, it does provide a purpose statement for all U.S. citizens. This new government would consist of the legislative, executive, and judicial branches of government. These are Articles 1-3 in your notes. These Articles are in place so that no one branch of government has absolute power because we all know that **absolute power corrupts absolutely**. So, the rulebook came with built in checks and balances.*

Remember, when you paraphrased the Preamble? Well, everything you said was true. Those are all things that are needed if someone is going to be together, united together. But what Ms. W didn't clarify was that as a black person, you weren't even considered a citizen when this Preamble was written. You see, as there are two sides of a coin – the north and the south, there are two sides of the legislative branch -- House of Representative and the Senate. The South wanted the state representatives to be based on population and the North wanted every state to have the same number of representatives. Having representation based on population was important to the South because that's where the majority of the slave owners resided, and in order to gain a political advantage, they would count slaves as a part of their population. Even though slaves had been classified as property, this was about a coin. This was for a political advantage. The compromise was that the House of Representatives would be based on the population of the state and the Senate would be have the same number of members (two delegates) for each state. However, only free people were to be counted as a whole, and slaves were to be counted as three-fifths of a person. This actually made it into the Constitution (Article 1, Section 2, Paragraph 3). There seemed to have been a lot of fractions being used back then. Anyway, this compromise gave Southern states strong political power. In fact, the majority of the presidential elections were won by slave owners. Slavery continued to be an issue that divided the North and South up through the Civil War.

Although the end of slavery is often considered an effect of the Civil War through the Emancipation Proclamation along with the Thirteenth, Fourteenth, and Fifteenth Amendments, slavery really did not end nor did the maltreatment of black people. About 30 years after the Civil War, the octoroon, Homer Plessy and several others decided to test the law. They wanted to see if the Constitution would really protect a black man's rights – Thirteenth and Fourteenth Amendments. When Plessy was found guilty, he knew where he stood. He knew his rights were not going to be protected. Seven out of eight of the Justices agreed that Plessy was guilty. Justice Henry Brown spoke for the majority, "A statute which implies merely a legal distinction between the white and colored race – a distinction which is founded in the color of the two races, and which must always exist so long as white men are distinguished from the other race by color." However, Justice John Harlan, from Kentucky, was the lone Justice who favored Plessy stated, "Our Constitution is color-blind, and neither knows nor tolerates classes among citizens." The decision of the majority acted as if separate could be equal. It breathed breathe into Jim Crow. Separate could never be equal.

Years later, it would take the likes of Charles Hamilton Houston, a lawyer and the NAACP Litigation Director and his protégé, Thurgood Marshall, to orchestrate a plan to prove that separate cannot be equal, and they used public education as a platform. These were two brothers. You're always talking about white men did everything, but there were plenty of brothers working on our behalf, however, the history books don't give them much airtime. Thurgood Marshall actually represented the Browns, which included more families than just Linda's, in the Brown v. The Board of Education Topeka, Kansas case. When this case won in the Supreme

Court, it wasn't just a win for public education but it was a win against the entire Jim Crow doctrine. This case was won in 1954, however Bern and I told you when desegregation occurred in Louisville, Kentucky.

Yep, remember it was the 1975-76 school year; it took over 20 years before there was a real attempt to desegregate schools in Louisville. Separate could never be equal. Look at your school today; the majority of the students in your classes are black and brown people. Your test scores are low, and you have the least experienced teachers at your school. Not to mention, the school is in the west end. Are the schools in your neighborhood equal to the schools in other neighborhoods? I think not. Let's talk about our city. Yep, it is highly segregated. In fact, I read a study recently that stated Louisville was in the top five of the most segregated cities in the U.S.

Let's let the coin fall flat on one side. This side feels like we need to go back to neighborhood schools, because of the money, the coinage it takes to bus children across the district and then the shortage of bus drivers. Heck, the data reveals that when bus drivers don't come to work, the routes that don't get picked up are in the west end. And this is supposed to support the notion of neighborhood schools. On the other side, people are against neighborhood schools because they know the schools in the poor neighborhoods are already at a deficit. They are already subpar. In some ways, they are already re-segregated as you said, J. So, in their view if Jefferson County was to go back to neighborhood schools, then you will definitely have full re-segregation. Let's toss this coin in the air to look from other angles. Maybe there is an alternative perspective that people should be considering. How about keeping busing, but not requiring students to sit on a bus for more than about 20 minutes. You know, when you go to Waggener next year, that's going to be a long bus ride for you, J?

So you see, all of this information

that you've been learning does include you. It's not about the fact that a bunch of white men created the Constitution. The fact is that it has already been done. It has already been set as the law of the land. It is up to you, it is up to us, it is up to the whole village to know what our rights are and to fight for those rights. You are going through so much because you were meant to be a mouthpiece for other young, black males. Learn what you need to learn, so you can speak intelligently.

YOUR BALL

I woke up to Mama rubbing my shoulder. "Hey baby!"

I sat up trying to get my eyes to focus. As she became clearer, I smiled and then squeezed her so tight as if I hadn't seen her for weeks. I kissed her on the cheek. *I love my Mama.*

"Jalen, I'm sorry that I just fouled out the other day. I talked to Nana and she made me realize that I didn't even listen to you. I just listened to what they said at that school. I didn't give you a chance." She drops her eyes and I think I see salt water falling from them.

"Mama—"

"No, son let me finish. I've never told

you why I named you Jalen. The name Jalen means healer. I knew when I told your daddy that I was pregnant and he reacted the way that he did that I would have to raise you alone. I was hurt and confused because he said that he loved me, but he wasn't ready to be a dad. When you were born, you were so vulnerable and beautiful , but at the same time you instantly healed me of any hurt. Jalen, I love you to the moon and back. You are my everything. I want to keep you little and not ever let you grow up because I want you all to myself. But now, I know that I must allow you to grow up because you have some other healing to do in the world. I just want you to know that I am your biggest supporter and cheerleader. You've been destined to bring healing and I must allow you to do that. I've scheduled a meeting with Mr. White and Ms. Windows. We're getting you back into school tomorrow and then the ball is in your court."

DUE PROCESS

Me, Mama, and Nana all showed up to TMMS on Thursday, Day 2 of my suspension. They all met first while I sat with the secretary. I could hear the crowd shouting, "DEFENSE, DEFENSE, DEFENSE." I don't know what all was said, but when I was called into the room I was allowed to give my version of what happened and has been happening in Ms. W's class. I explained how Ms. W does not know how to teach and how she has to use her iPad for ideas. Then, I explained how boring the class is when we have to just sit there and wait. But the best part of my closing statement was, "Ms. W wants us to be patient with her while she is still learning to teach, but she does not give us the same patience back."

When I finished, Mama said, "See, my son's due process was totally ignored in this situation. His constitutional rights aren't dropped off at the school door, but they enter the school with him. He has equal protection of the law."

Mr. White and Ms. W did not say a word for several minutes and then, after the silence became awkward, Mr. White said, "Well, we'll drop the suspension for now. Jalen may return to class today."

WRITING RIGHTS

I had already missed Ms. W's class, but I attended my other classes. I asked my classmates what I had missed in Ms. W's class, and they said there was going to be a test tomorrow. That night, Mama let me get on the computer, and I studied the Constitution along with some of the stuff that Mama and E told me about.

The next day, I discovered the test was an essay test. It was a writing test. Awww man, I was expecting multiple guess. I had to write on how the Constitution is at work in my own life. Ms. W told us that a community organization had a writing contest going on about the Constitution, so she decided that she would enter our papers into the contest and make them count as a test grade. It seems like as I was writing stuff down that everything I had been taught came flowing back to me. I was on a roll.

Within a few days, I received my grade back from Ms. W. It was the same old, same old…a big red B. No explanation. No nothing. She grades based on her feelings of students and not based on what they did or did not do. She always in her feelings when it comes to me.

But, the glory came when Ms. W's face changed from a smile to frown as she read some letter.

Dear Ms. Windows:

> *It is with great honor that we announce Jalen Williams' essay is the $500 winner of our essay contest. Jalen's essay embodied all of the*

elements that we respect and honor in our youth – honesty, integrity, and solution-oriented. We can clearly see all of the things that you have been teaching this young man! He masterfully detailed his expansive knowledge concerning rights. We would like to present him with his award at the eighth grade graduation next week and we ask that he be allowed to share just a portion of this great essay!

Sincerely,

Matt Matheison
Rotary Club #123

Mama told me not to spend so much time concentrating on Ms. W and to stay focused with my own stuff, so I quit looking at her after I noticed she suddenly became mad. When the bell rang, Ms. W asked me to stay after for a minute or two. *What have I done now? This is getting on my nerves. I'm trying to keep to myself.*

"Well, Jalen, apparently the Rotary Club has named you the winner of the essay contest. They want you to read a portion of your essay at the eighth grade graduation."

I stood there unable to speak, then I had to know so I asked, "Are you sure it's my essay that they liked?"

"Yes, I am sure."

WE MUST OVERCOME

Our past and our future meet today, in the present. We are in this thing together, and in order for us to have a decent home to hand over to our future, we must heal the things that have separated us. Separate is not equal. Separate is not fair. There is no liberty in separation. Division means two visions, two sides. We are one unit. We are one coin. We are invaluable as one. Devalued as fractional pieces. We cannot allow hate, power, or money make us into things that we cannot be proud of when they read about us in history.

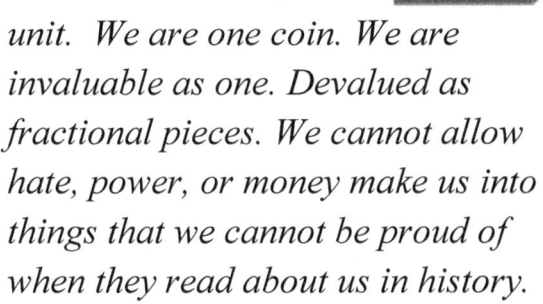

On my journey, I have heard about

heroes both black and white from our history. They were not heroes because the history books named them as such, but they are heroes because they stood up when others wanted them to shut up. Some of you may have heard of Homer Plessy, John Harlan, Linda Brown, Charles Houston, and Thurgood Marshall, but others are just regular common people like Eric Johnson, Bern O'Connell, my mama, and my nana. They are my heroes. They are courageous people who stood in the face of adversity because they knew the land needed to be healed and they were willing to leave their places of comfort to reach into the dark, lonely place of discomfort. These are giants whose shoulders I have stood on to find my way. Today, I have found my way.

Swish. The audience stood up and applauded me. *All net*. I smile cause I know where I came from and I realize I've grown. I'm not what I want to be, but I ain't who I used to be either. As I leave the podium to go hug my Mama and Nana, someone taps me on my shoulder. I turn around and it is this old bruh, maybe fifty years old or something, he says, "Great job, J! I'm proud of you." Then he winks at me. Before I can respond, my Mama runs up to me; she hugs me as she cries into my ear. I cry, too, but I cry in my mother's chest so that no one will think I'm a punk. Then, I hear that song that Nana sings when she needs a bit of encouragement. You know the one, the one about overcoming. After all the hugging and kissing, I realize I'm starving. Before I can even tell Mama that I'm ready to go eat, she says, "Jalen, where do you want to go to eat to celebrate your graduation?"

At that moment, I spot Malachi. I leave Mama's side to run over to hug and congratulate him, "Hey Malachi, where do you want to eat?"

He pulls out a quarter, "Call it, heads or tails."

"I call heads."

He tosses the coin into the air and it does it rotating thing. It falls on the ground and lands with tails showing. Malachi grins his famous grin because it never falls on tails, "I guess it's Cheesecake Factory, bruh."

"I guess so."

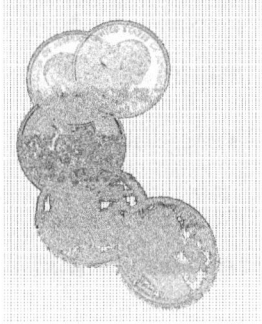

ABOUT THE AUTHOR

Dr. Kimberly Mucker-Johnson has been an educator for over 15 years. She currently serves as an Instructional Coach in an urban school district in Kentucky. In addition, she is currently working on a degree and state licensure in mental health counseling.

Dr. Mucker-Johnson lives in Louisville, Kentucky. She is married to Eric and has two sons, Derrick and Keonte'.

www.ingramcontent.com/pod-product-compliance
Lightning Source LLC
LaVergne TN
LVHW051606070426
835507LV00021B/2801